At a Glance™ Series

DVD and Lesson Book

DVD Guitar Licks

Written by Andrew DuBrock, Chad Johnson & Michael Mueller
Video Performers: Wolf Marshall, Troy Stetina & Tom Kolb

ISBN: 978-1-4234-6223-1

HAL•LEONARD®
CORPORATION
7777 W. BLUEMOUND RD. P.O. BOX 13819 MILWAUKEE, WI 53213

Visit Hal Leonard Online at
www.halleonard.com

Table of Contents

Introduction

Great lead guitarists often seem like magicians, effortlessly pulling cool solos out of their hat. But while these spectacular leads seem to come out of thin air, they are usually based on *something*. Many guitarists sculpt their lines from *licks* they've picked up from their heroes, friends, and even other instruments. Licks can be short, long, down at the nut, or even span all the way across the fretboard. Licks find their way into nearly every genre—from smoking blues players like Robben Ford, to revolutionary rockers like Eddie Van Halen, to blues legends like Freddie King and country icons like Chet Atkins. As a student of guitar licks, learn all the cool licks you can get your hands on. Then, try and integrate them into your own playing. True lick masters find ways of twisting, shaping, and joining licks in new ways to create their own unique licks and riffs.

Now, to get all those licks under your belt, you have to start *playing*, not reading endless texts. If traditional method books put you to sleep, this book will wake you up and get you playing. From Hal Leonard's exciting new At a Glance series, *Guitar Licks* is presented in a snappy and fun manner intended to have you playing licks and solos in virtually no time at all. Plus, the At a Glance series uses real riffs and licks by real artists to illustrate how the concepts you're learning are applied in top-selling songs. For example, in *Guitar Licks*, you'll learn riffs and solo licks from such classics as Eric Clapton's "Cross Road Blues," The Beatles' "All My Loving," AC/DC's "Back in Black," and Van Halen's "You Really Got Me," to name just a few.

Additionally, each book in the At a Glance series comes with a DVD containing video lessons that correspond to the printed material. The DVD that accompanies this book contains four video lessons, each approximately 8 to 10 minutes in length, that correspond to the topics covered in *Guitar Licks*. In these videos, masters lick navigators Troy Stetina, Tom Kolb, and Wolf Marshall will show you in great detail everything from how to play open-position licks to expertly connecting minor and major pentatonic scales within licks. As you work your way through *Guitar Licks*, try to play the examples first on your own, and then check out the DVD for additional help or to see if you played it correctly. As the saying goes, "A picture is worth a thousand words," so be sure to use this invaluable tool on your quest to becoming a lick master.

ROCK LICKS

Rock music wouldn't be half as exciting without the lead guitar. In this lesson, we'll look at the techniques and concepts used by some of rock's most influential soloists in their *rock licks*. Rock licks can use slides, hammer-ons, pull-offs, and many other techniques, but aside from specific techniques, many rock licks are built from specific *scales*.

Scales

We'll start by looking at some of the scales that are commonly used in most rock licks. If any of these are new to you, you might want to brush up on them a bit before tackling the licks in this lesson.

Minor Pentatonic/Blues Scale

The first scale we'll look at is the good old *minor pentatonic scale*. Here's the A minor pentatonic scale:

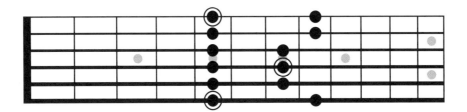

A close relative to the minor pentatonic, here's the A blues scale, which just adds the ♭5th:

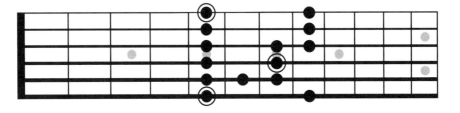

Major Pentatonic Scale

Next up is the *major pentatonic scale*. The A major pentatonic scale looks like this:

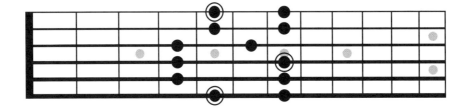

Dorian Mode

Next we have the *Dorian mode*, which is just like a minor scale, except it has a major 6th. Here's A Dorian:

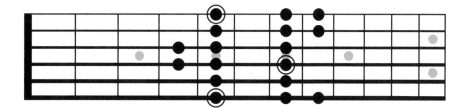

Natural Minor Scale (Aeolian Mode)

Finally, here's the *natural minor scale*, which is also known as the *Aeolian mode*. Here's the A natural minor scale:

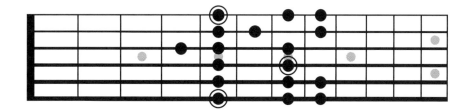

There are definitely others, but that's plenty for us to work with for now. Remember that all these scale forms are moveable for playing in whatever key you want. Also realize that several of these scales may be combined in one lick, as we'll soon see.

Early Rock 'N' Roll

Rock has evolved quite a bit throughout the years, so we're going to group the licks in this lesson by general time period. We'll start with early rock 'n' roll, which was epitomized by players like Chuck Berry and Scotty Moore.

This first lick is based off the classic Chuck Berry intro lick. It's in the key of A.

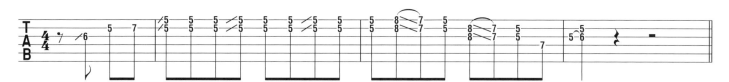

Here's a similar idea in G that features bent double-stops—a common device in this style.

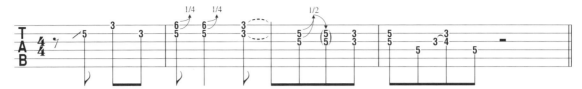

And here's another classic bending move, this time in C. The first part of this lick can be repeated as long as you like.

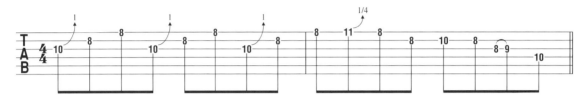

Here's Chuck Berry's lick in the opening measures of "The Promised Land." Note how similar this lick is to our earlier Chuck Berry riff. The main difference here is that Berry moves his pattern up to the eighth fret to play in the key of C.

Words and Music by
Chuck Berry

N.C.

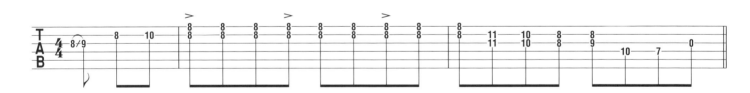

'60s ROCK

With sixties rock, we find, of course, Jimi Hendrix, and other giants like Eric Clapton and Jeff Beck. The licks in this era exploited greater amp sustain and also showed an increase in technical facility.

The *unison bend* was a commonly used technique of the day; here it is in an E minor pentatonic lick:

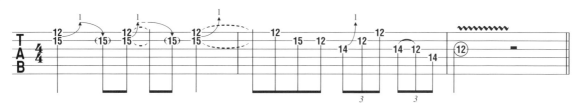

Clapton is famous for his smooth, speedy blues licks with Cream—like this lick in A:

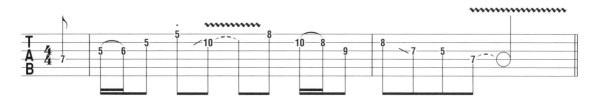

Hendrix was known for, among other things, his speedy pentatonic flourishes, like this one in C# minor pentatonic.

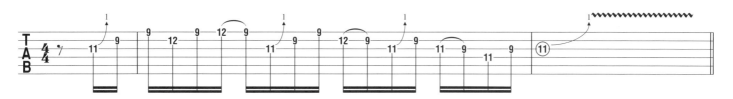

Here's a real-world example of a '60s rock lick. This fill, from Cream's "White Room," shows Eric Clapton expertly navigating through the minor pentatonic scale to coax a slippery lick from his guitar. Note how the slide down to the lower minor pentatonic position and back up again in the second measure contribute to the smooth and slippery feel.

"WHITE ROOM"
Cream

Words and Music by Jack Bruce
and Pete Brown

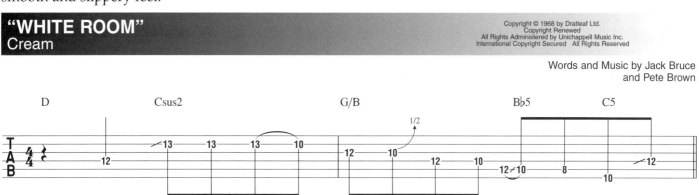

'70s ROCK

Although disco ruled much of the seventies, there were still plenty of guitar slingers around—namely Jimmy Page, Peter Frampton, Ted Nugent, and the like. The rock of this decade was big and loud, and the licks followed suit.

Flashy, repetitive licks were popular, like this one from the E minor pentatonic box.

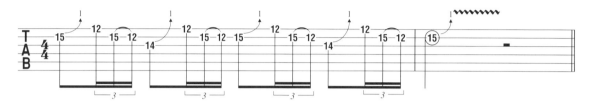

This one, in the style of Page, uses rapid open-string pull-offs, which were common as well.

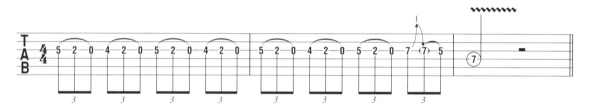

Duane Allman used a similar lick in the Allman Brothers Band's epic live recording of "Whipping Post," from *Live at Fillmore East*. Check out how he plays his lick on *two* strings, alternating between the third and fourth strings.

"WHIPPING POST"
Allman Brothers Band

Words and Music by
Gregg Allman

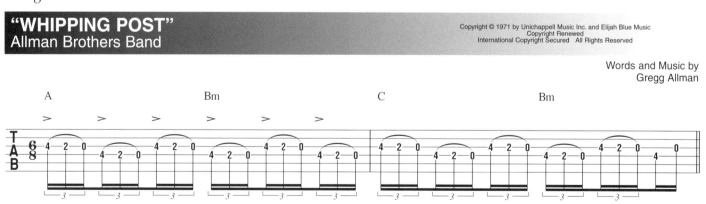

Funk influenced the solos of the day as well, as demonstrated in this Frampton-style lick in D.

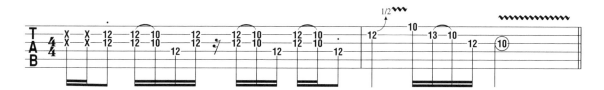

MODERN ROCK

We'll think of everything from the eighties on as modern rock, since the guitar solo essentially reached its peak in the eighties.

Flash was definitely the name of the game (and, of course, big hair). Three-note-per-string patterns became very popular, and this Van Halen-type lick uses a legato technique to breeze through one in B Dorian.

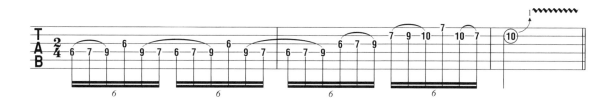

Hammer-ons and pull-offs drive the legato feel of the previous example; Van Halen makes his legato technique even more fluid by tapping on the fretboard with his picking hand. This excerpt, from his solo on "You Really Got Me," shows Van Halen really strutting his stuff. Watch out for all the fret-hand tapping here. The only notes you'll actually pick (with your guitar pick instead of tapping) are at the beginning of the lick and for the bend on the fourth fret of the third string.

"YOU REALLY GOT ME"
Van Halen

Words and Music by
Ray Davies

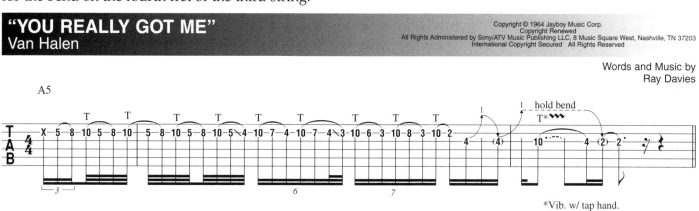

*Vib. w/ tap hand.

Alternately picking every note results in a very aggressive sound, as demonstrated in this A minor pentatonic lick.

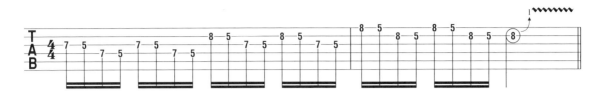

This speedy lick in E Dorian incorporates a bit of a left-hand stretch.

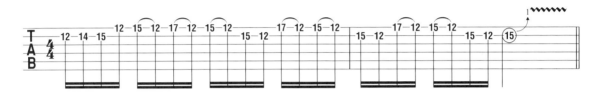

This super-fast lick, from Whitesnake's "Here I Go Again," runs up the G major scale over a C chord—all in the key of G. To keep stretches to a minimum, break things down into three-note groups and shift your hand after each three-note set. For instance, on the first beat, grab the eighth fret with your index finger and follow that up with your middle and pinky fingers on the tenth and twelfth frets, respectively. Then, slide that finger combination up to the tenth fret for the next three notes, and continue up the fretboard in the same way.

"HERE I GO AGAIN"
Whitesnake

Words and Music by Bernie Marsden
and David Coverdale

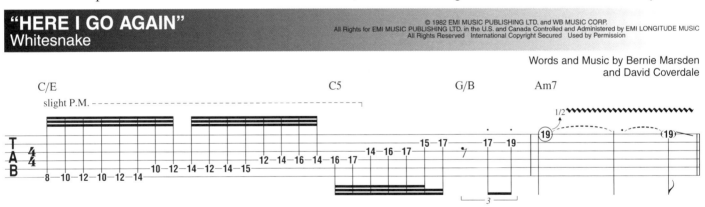

OPEN-POSITION LICKS

Mention the phrase "open-position" to a guitar player, and odds are good that the first things that come to mind are beginner's lessons or strumming cowboy chords. But considering some of the greatest guitar licks ever played have come from those first few frets and open strings, that's an unfair assessment. In this lesson, we'll show you sixteen classic open licks from blues, rock, country, and bluegrass legends. So grab your flatpick and prepare to ring some strings!

Blues Licks

From the pioneering acoustic bluesmen like Charley Patton and Robert Johnson, to the early electric blues of Muddy Waters and John Lee Hooker, to modern masters like Stevie Ray Vaughan and Joe Bonamassa, the guitar's open position has been a breeding ground for timeless blues licks.

 This first lick, an E minor pentatonic line played over an E7 chord, is heard in various forms in the work of John Lee Hooker, Muddy Waters, and countless others.

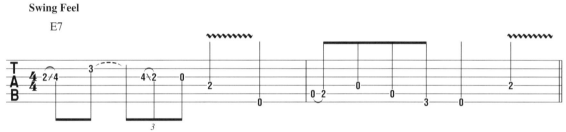

 Our second open-position blues lick, also played over an E7 chord, builds on the foundation of our previous lick, adding the bluesy ♭5th and a cool trill. This "chopsy" lick is in the style of the great blues technicians Stevie Ray Vaughan and Joe Bonamassa.

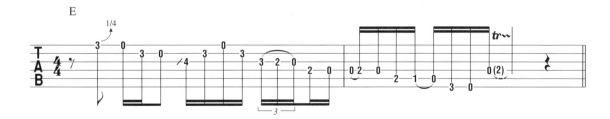

The rhythms in this lick might prove a bit tricky at first, so start slowly and get the feel right.

Our next open-position blues lick offers up a cool major tonality over E7. Inspired by the Texas Cannonball, Freddie King, the lick draws from the E major pentatonic scale in the first bar and first beat of the second bar, before switching to the combined E major-minor pentatonic scale for the closing phrase.

Swing feel

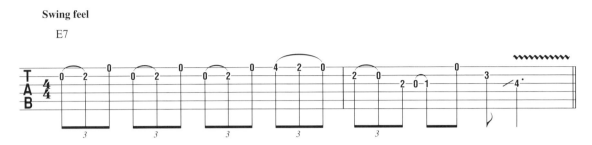

Blues legend Stevie Ray Vaughan kicks off his tune "Pride and Joy" in the open position—including this fiery lick down at the nut. Check out how he slides briefly to the extended box shape at the beginning of the lick, then slides back down to hammer and pull notes from the E minor pentatonic scale, adding just the right touch of bluesiness with the $\flat$5 (B$\flat$, taken from the E blues scale), but tempered with the major seventh (D$\sharp$, taken from the major scale).

"PRIDE AND JOY"
Stevie Ray Vaughan

Written by Stevie Ray Vaughan

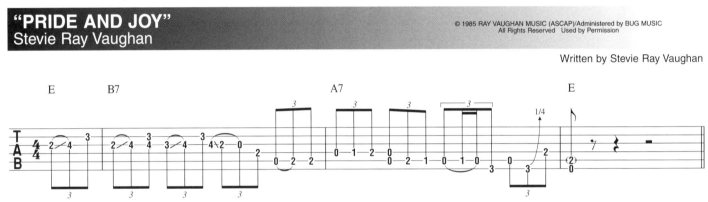

Rock Licks

Borrowing largely from the blues world, rock guitarists—especially classic rockers—are also quite capable of exploiting the first five frets on the guitar. It should be noted that most of the open-position rock licks you hear are likely being played over an Em, E5, or E7 chord, so we're going to focus exclusively on rock licks in E.

Our first rock lick is in the style of the great Jimi Hendrix, one of the most exciting open-position rock guitarists ever. For a change of pace, this lick in E is in 12/8 time, a favorite slow blues vehicle for Hendrix. Dig the D-to-E trill that closes the lick—another favorite move of Hendrix.

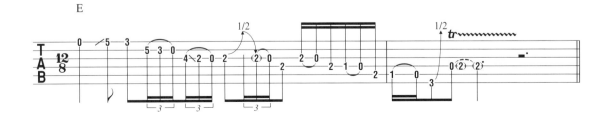

If you're not comfortable counting rhythm in 12/8, try thinking of it as four beats of eighth-note triplets.

This next example shows Hendrix in action with his tasty intro lick to "Hey Joe." Notice how he heads up the fretboard briefly to grab partial chord shapes over open strings and finishes with a huge E5 power chord.

"HEY JOE"
Jimi Hendrix

Words and Music by
Billy Roberts

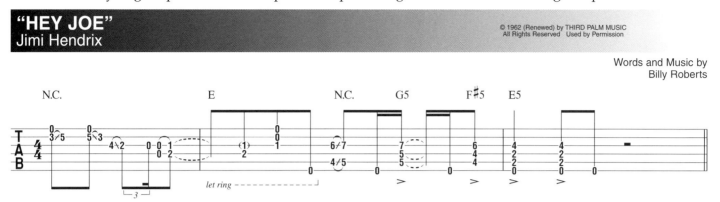

Creedence Clearwater Revival open their classic tune "Green River" with a nifty hybrid-picked open-position lick. As you can see, a common theme in many of these open-position licks is sliding up to that extended blues box shape (here on beat 2 of the first measure). Many guitarists slide up to this box by using their index and ring fingers for the third and fourth frets, respectively. But, in this case, you'll need to use your middle and ring fingers so that you can still fret that second-fret E note on beats 3 and 4 with your index finger.

"GREEN RIVER"
Creedence Clearwater Revival

Words and Music by
John Fogerty

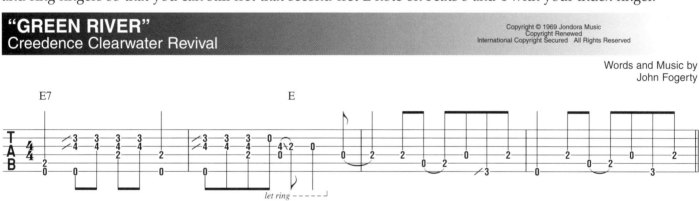

Led Zeppelin's Jimmy Page is a master riffer, and his short, bluesy licks reflect his knack for gritty hooks. This lick comes straight out of the E blues scale, with a tension-raising slow bend up to the 5th to cap it all off.

Swing feel

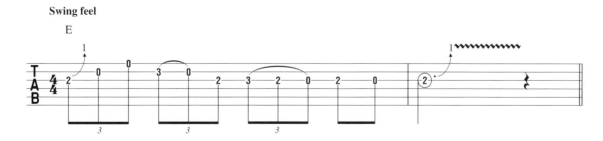

Our next rock lick comes from down under. Aussie rockers AC/DC have made a career of pounding out open-position power chords, and lead guitarist Angus Young knows just what to do with those big E5 chords.

In this lick, rather than sticking to the E minor pentatonic scale, we're going hybrid, adding in the 6th, C#, and the 9th, F#, for added flair.

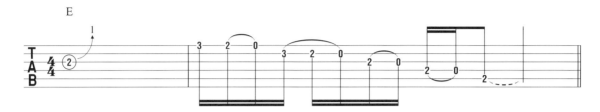

AC/DC have a knack for creating memorable riffs to anchor every song. In the signature riff for "Back in Black," check how they inject life into the chord-based riff with the slinky open-position lick in measures 2.

"BACK IN BLACK"
AC/DC

Words and Music by Angus Young,
Malcolm Young and Brian Johnson

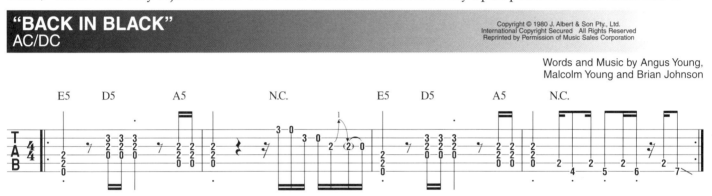

Country Licks

Hot country guitar was born when fretburners like Jimmy Bryant, Joe Maphis, and even Chet Atkins took to playing fiddle tunes on the guitar—mostly in open position. A good number of country licks are played in the keys of G, C, and A, as those are the most popular country keys.

Our first lick is a descending gem culled from the blues/Mixolydian hybrid scale.

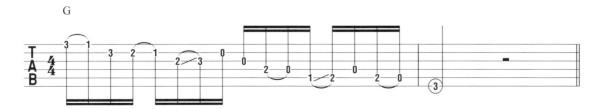

This next lick is a slippery-sounding legato line in the key of C. Be sure you don't rush the slides at the start of the lick.

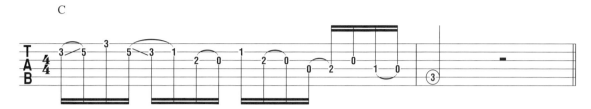

Our third country lick is a Chet Atkins-inspired barn burner. This phrase entails a descending sequence of triplet pull-offs to open strings.

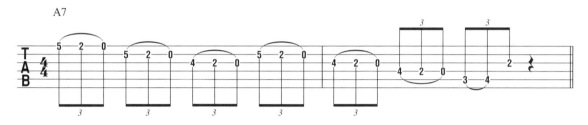

These types of fast pull-off licks are easy ones to rush, so pay strict attention to your time.

Now here's Chet Atkins smoking things up in the intro to "Big Foot." Check out how this supercharged lick switches from an A major to an A Mixolydian sound midway through with the addition of the open G string. Though this sounds and feels like an open-position lick (due to all those open strings and your proximity to the nut), you'll actually want to park your fingers in second position, assigning one finger per fret from strings 2–5. In this formation, you should be able to navigate all of those hammer-ons and pull-offs with ease, though you might get a speeding ticket!

"BIG FOOT"
Chet Atkins

Written by Chet Atkins

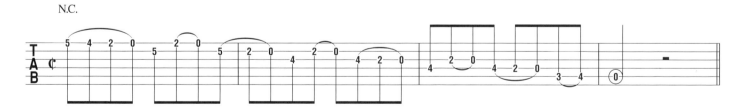

Bluegrass Licks

The last two licks in this lesson come from the bluegrass world. With much of its repertoire coming from traditional fiddle tunes, it's little surprise that bluegrass guitarists are among the most proficient open-position flatpickers you'll find. Guitarist Lester Flatt, of the legendary bluegrass duo of Flatt and Scruggs, devised this first lick and played it so famously that it's become known as the Lester Flatt run. Here it is, in the key of G.

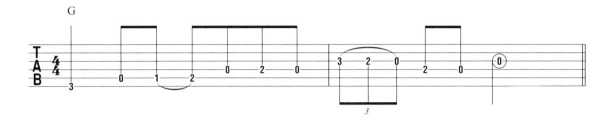

Our final lick comes from bluegrass guitar legend Doc Watson. Culled from the C major blues scale, this line craftily inserts the ♭3rd as a passing tone twice in its descent.

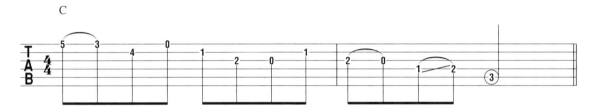

For easiest execution, begin the lick with your hand in third position and immediately shift down to open position on the "and" of beat 2.

Well, there you have it: sixteen licks from four different genres with the singular purpose of showing you that there's a whole lot more to the open position than strumming folk tunes! Regardless of the style of music you play, next time you're improvising, give some love to those first few frets and open strings, and your reward will ring out loud and proud.

DOUBLE STOPS

In this lesson, we're going to look at double stops and how players apply them to riffs and solos. We'll learn some great licks in different styles along the way and see why this technique has become a mainstay in the guitar world.

Technically, a double stop is created when two notes are played at the same time. Double stops on adjacent strings are probably the most common, such as these:

But non-adjacent strings can be used too, as we can see here:

Regarding the right hand, almost all the examples in this lesson can be played with a pick or fingers, or, you could use both, which is called hybrid picking. You might want to experiment and see which method or methods you prefer.

The Minor Pentatonic Scale Shape

To get started, let's apply double stops to a scale shape we're probably all very familiar with: the minor pentatonic scale. For clarification, here's the shape in A minor:

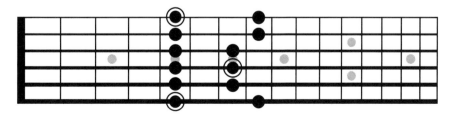

Now let's play the shape in double stops. In other words, you'll be playing through the shape two strings at a time. It looks like this:

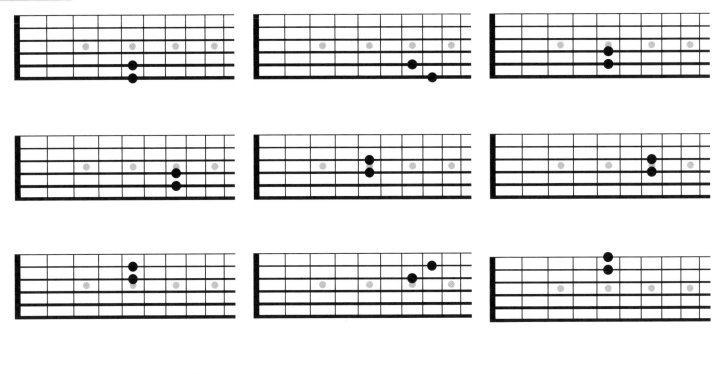

With the exception of the second and seventh double stops we just played (shown below)—which are major 3rds—every other double stop we played was a 4th.

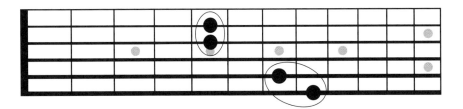

This creates a powerful sound that can be used to thicken up a normal line. For example, take this line:

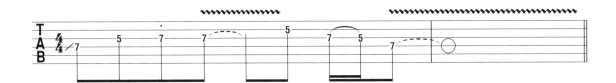

You could play it as a double-stop line for a different effect, like this:

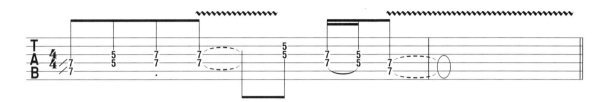

Or, try this single-note line:

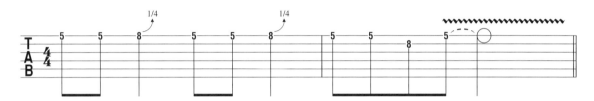

With double stops, it would sound like this:

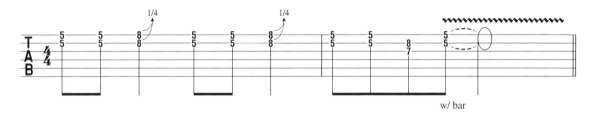

You'll find this technique cropping up within virtually every style and genre in the book. Here's an example of how the Offspring used double-stop combinations as a lead lick in their hit "Come Out and Play."

"COME OUT AND PLAY"
The Offspring

Words and Music by
Dexter Holland

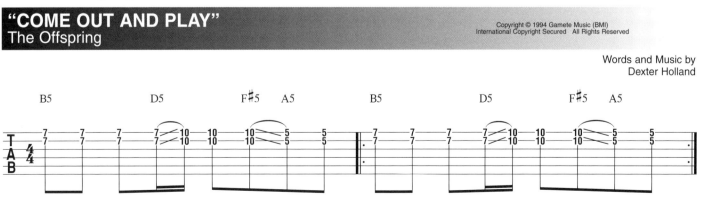

The Dorian/Blues Scale Combination

A very common approach with double stops involves the Dorian mode mixed with the blues scale. That may sound complicated, but this is all we're talking about:

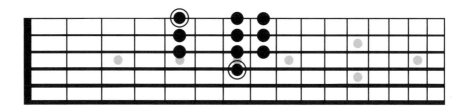

When we play the double stops from this shape, we get this:

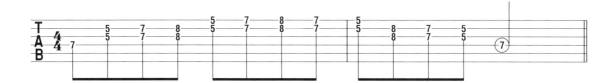

This little shape has been used in countless riffs throughout the years—things like this:

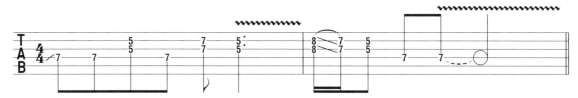

Now, when you add the major 3rd to this shape, you've got all the ingredients needed to play some great Chuck Berry-style licks.

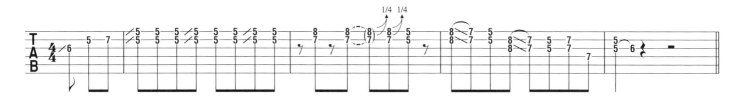

Or you can try out some old Delta-blues style things:

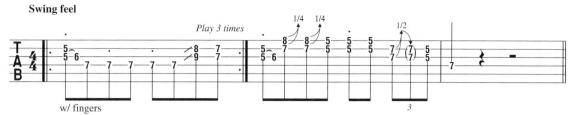

You can hear Stevie Ray Vaughan's take on these Chuck Berry-style licks in "Love Struck Baby," where he wraps up each 12-bar chorus in his solo with similar licks from this shape.

"LOVE STRUCK BABY"
Stevie Ray Vaughan

Written by Stevie Ray Vaughan

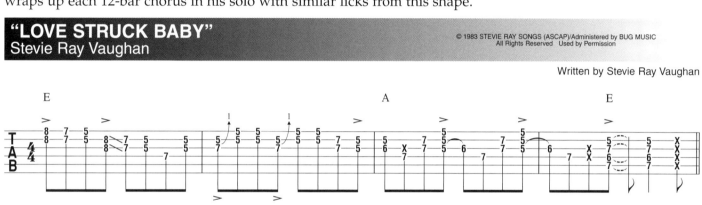

Blues Turnaround Licks

Speaking of Delta blues, double stops are perfect for turnaround licks. Here are four variations on a turnaround in G using double stops. This first one uses chromatically descending 3rds.

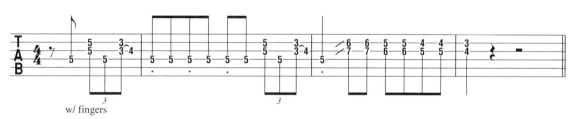

Here we're descending chromatically with 6ths.

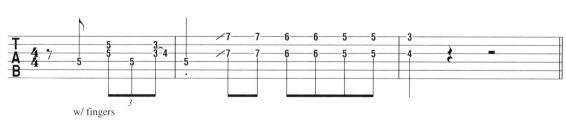

More chromatic 6ths.

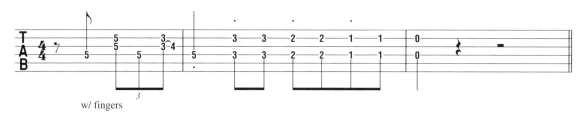

And this last one uses a pedal point on top—a high G note.

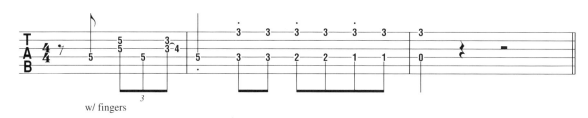

There are lots of variations on these basic turnaround ideas. Experiment with them and see what else you can come up with—you can never know too many turnaround licks!

Motown Rhythm Style

Another style where double stops are constantly used is the Motown/R&B style, which was popularized by players like Steve Cropper and Curtis Mayfield. Hendrix built on this style and made it a big part of his rhythm playing. It involves sliding, hammering on, or pulling off double stops around certain chord shapes. The most common double stops used are 3rds, 4ths, and 6ths, but other intervals can be used too.

Let's start with this G chord barre shape:

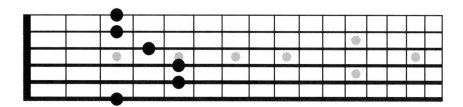

Now we'll take a look at some typical embellishments we might play in this style.

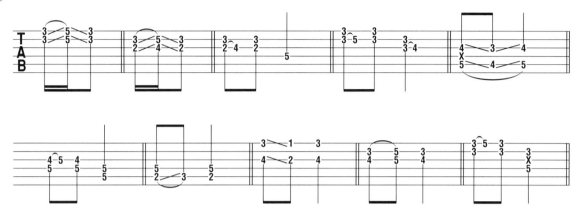

You can mix and match all these embellishments to create some very interesting rhythm parts that are fun to play. You might come up with something like this:

N.C.(G)

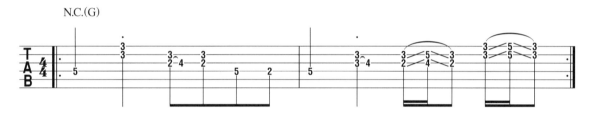

Or maybe something a little funkier:

N.C.(G7)

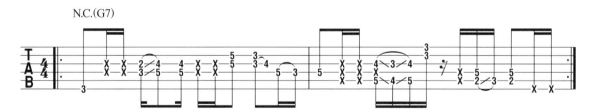

By sliding some 6ths around on the higher strings, you can get some of those great Steve Cropper-type riffs.

N.C.(G7)   (C)

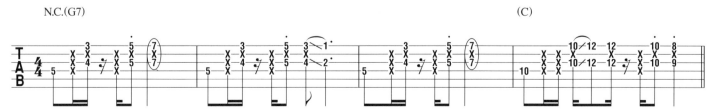

Rock Double Stops

Double stops have been used throughout the history of rock music, in nearly every sub-genre you can imagine. The Beatles—probably the most popular pop-rock band of all time—used double stops from the beginning of their careers. In their 1963 hit "All My Loving," George Harrison crafted a melodic solo using double-stop sixth and fifth intervals.

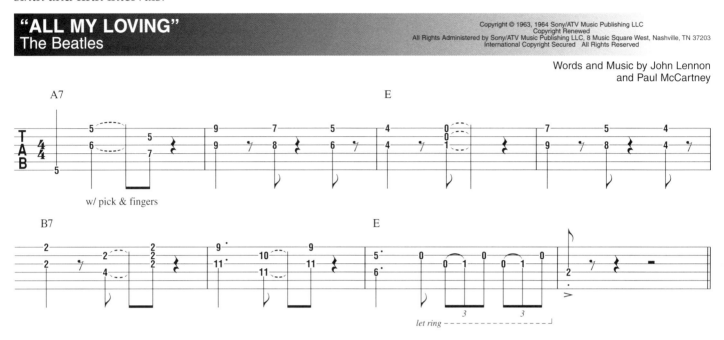

Four years later, Van Morrison made his mark with "Brown Eyed Girl"—a pop gem anchored by a catchy double-stop lick in thirds.

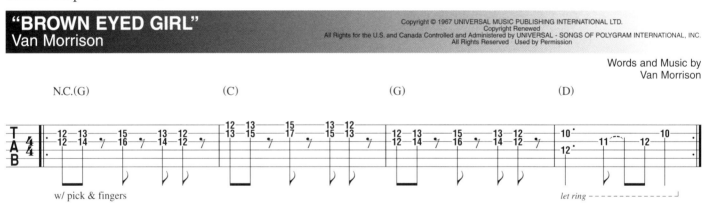

Fast forward to 2004, and Los Lonely Boys had a funky pop-rock hit with "Heaven." Like Van Morrison, they used double-stop thirds to create their signature lick. But, instead of jumping between string sets like Morrison did, they opted to slide up and down the first two strings to keep the funky, sliding feel alive.

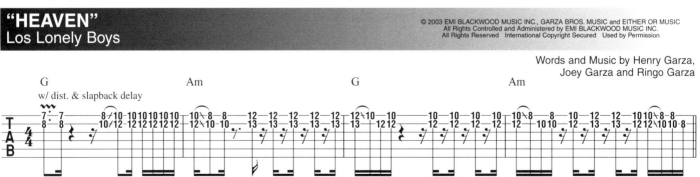

Chances are that you could pick out any year on your calendar and find a multitude of hits (and bombs too…) that use double stops of all kinds.

Major Scale Double-Stop Exercise

There's a great exercise you can do that will really help you learn the most commonly used double stops all over the neck. First, pick a key. Let's say we're going to use G major. Start on the two highest strings and play through the notes of the G major scale in 3rds—all the way from the lowest position you can find up until you span an octave.

In our case, the lowest 3rd in the key of G on the first two strings is the first fret of the second string (C) and the open first string (E), so we'll start there. It will look like this:

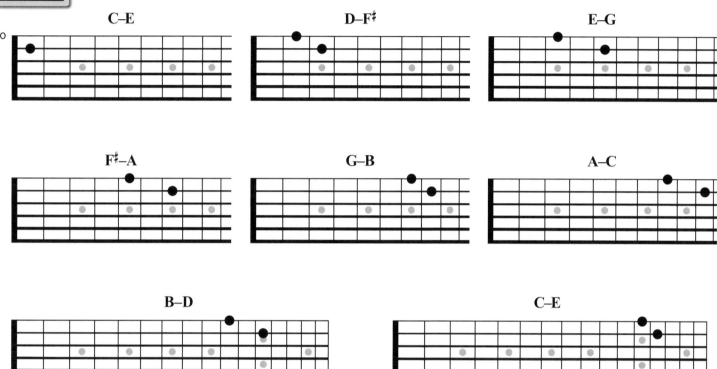

Basically, you're playing a major scale all on one string, but you're doing it two strings at a time in 3rds. Do this on every set of two adjacent strings:

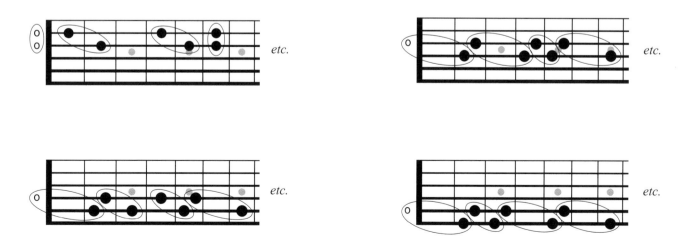

Continue on up to the twelfth fret on all of these string sets.

Now do the same thing with 6ths, starting with the first and third strings.

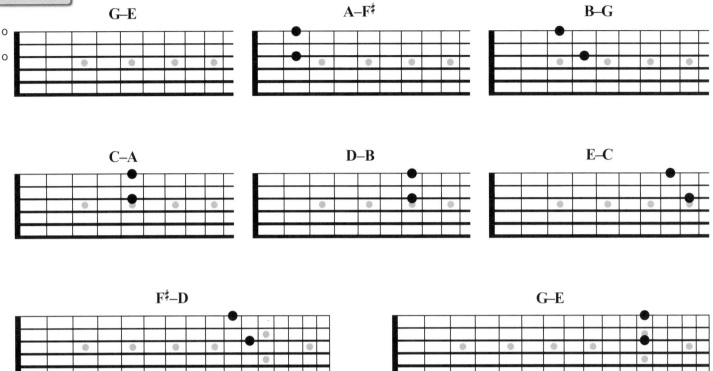

And then move to each other set of strings.

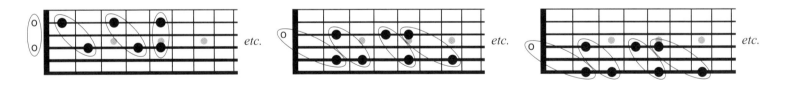

You can do this with any interval you'd like: 4ths, 5ths, 7ths, etc. After you get through all the intervals, change keys. You might work on a new key every day or two until you've covered all twelve keys. By the time you've done all that, you'll know your double stops all over the neck and will be able to throw them into your riffs or solos any time you like.

COMBINING MAJOR AND MINOR PENTATONICS

When guitar players begin learning improvisation, the minor pentatonic is typically the first scale mastered. Later, they may discover the major pentatonic, particularly if they have an interest in Southern rock or country music, but few guitarists take the time to learn how to effectively mix major and minor pentatonic sounds. For those adventurous few, a fabulous reward awaits. In this lesson, we're going to explore the art of combining the major and minor pentatonic scales to create exciting new licks and phrases.

Let's start with a quick review of these two basic scales.

Minor Pentatonic Scale

The minor pentatonic is a five-note scale containing the root, ♭3rd, 4th, 5th, and ♭7th degrees of the major scale. There are five fingering patterns available across the fretboard. Here's the most popular—in root position—in the key of A minor.

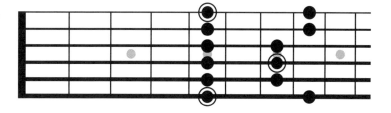

Major Pentatonic Scale

The major pentatonic is also a five-note scale, and it contains the root, 2nd, 3rd, 5th, and 6th degrees of the major scale. Like the minor pentatonic, the major pentatonic scale also has five fingering patterns across the fretboard. Here's the root-position shape in the key of A major.

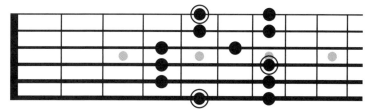

Major-Minor Mix Scale

Now we come to the fun part. When you combine the major and minor pentatonic scales, you get an eight-note scale with the same notes as the Mixolydian mode, plus a ♭3rd. Here's a fingering pattern for this combined scale.

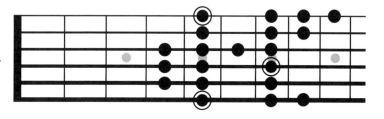

While that may seem like a lot of notes for one scale, you won't be using it to perform root-to-octave scale runs. Rather, the combined major-minor pentatonic scale is typically employed as a major or minor pentatonic scale would be, using the extra notes as color tones. Now, let's take a look at some phrasing applications.

Major-Minor Ambiguity

First of all, because combining the major and minor pentatonic scales results in the Mixolydian mode plus a ♭3rd, it's a great scale to use over dominant chords. And, because the combined scale contains both a major and minor 3rd degree, you can choose between minor-sounding, major-sounding, or tonally ambiguous licks.

 For example, here's a cool lick in A that feels neither major nor minor.

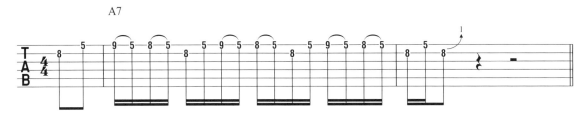

As both the C and the C♯, which are the ♭3rd and 3rd, respectively, are key to the lick, its tonality is ambiguous.

The Major-Minor Rub

Conversely, combining the major and minor pentatonic scales also offers the opportunity to truly exploit what we call the major-minor rub, thus creating tremendous tension and release.

 Here's a lick over G13 designed to do just that, with its B♭ to B hammer-on move near the end.

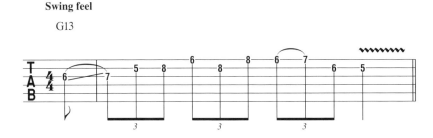

The "Hendrix Chord"

Think about it: combining the major and minor pentatonic scales results in the Mixolydian mode plus a ♭3rd, which is enharmonically equivalent to the ♯9th. This in turn makes it the *perfect* scale for soloing over a dominant 7♯9 chord, popularly known as the "Hendrix chord."

 Here's an example. This lick also adds a ♭5th for extra bluesiness.

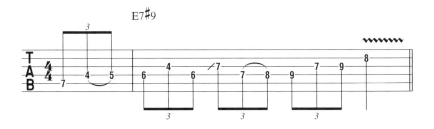

Mix Masters

For more examples of how to effectively combine these two scales, let's take a look at some of the masters of the mix. As this scale is most commonly found in blues-rock, we're going to keep our focus there.

Eric Clapton

As the man who practically invented blues-rock guitar, Eric Clapton set the bar for mixing major and minor pentatonic scales higher than the heavens, with his timeless work in Cream.

Here's an example of his masterly mixing.

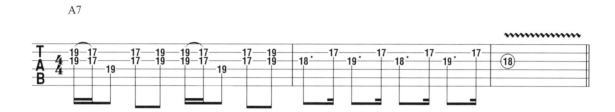

Note that the first bar is minor pentatonic with an added 6th, and the second is major pentatonic with an added 4th.

Clapton alternated so effortlessly between major and minor pentatonic scale patterns in his legendary "Cross Road Blues" solo that he created countless must-know licks in one solo alone! Here's just one of many examples found throughout this solo. This one finds Clapton stringing several licks together as he navigates way up at the 17th–20th frets to close out his screaming second solo. Note how he starts off with the minor pentatonic scale, only first hinting at the major pentatonic scale with the half-step bend to the major 3rd at the end of measure 2. In measure three, he again briefly touches on the major sound with a hammer on to the 3rd, but by the fourth measures he's shifted completely over to the major pentatonic scale for a classic old-school blues move. Then he skillfully shifts back to the minor pentatonic scale in the sixth measure, finishing the solo with some rapid-fire moves (adding just a hint of major with that major 3rd in the final measure).

"CROSS ROAD BLUES" (CROSSROADS)
Cream

Words and Music by
Robert Johnson

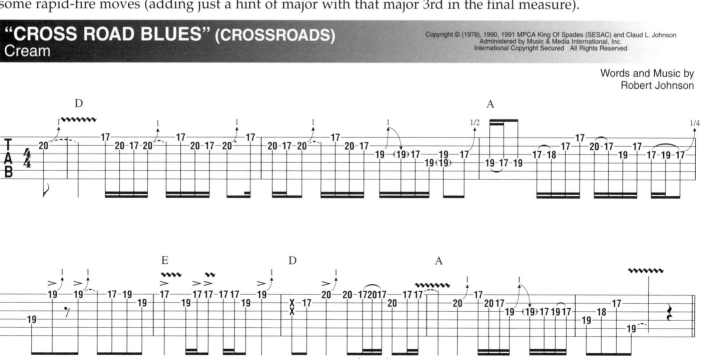

Joe Perry

Like Clapton, Aerosmith guitarist Joe Perry has a sound and style all his own. Much of what sets him apart from other blues-rockers is his phrasing, often drawing from both the major and minor pentatonic scales to craft his lines.

Here's a Perry-esque syncopated double-stop lick that fully exploits the major minor rub over an A7 chord.

The syncopation looks and sounds tricky, but it's pretty easy if you start slow and get it right from the start.

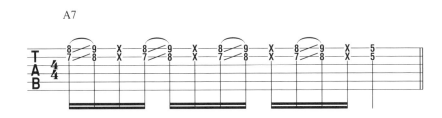

Here's another lick that Perry plays to close out his solo in "Same old Song and Dance." Perry starts off playing E minor pentatonic, but quickly shifts to a mixed scale with the G♯ on the and of beat 4, navigating through the mix for a full measure before returning to the minor pentatonic scale.

"SAME OLD SONG AND DANCE"
Aerosmith

Words and Music by Steven Tyler
and Joe Perry

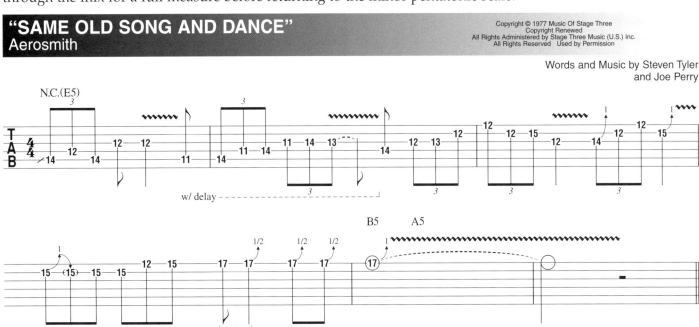

Black Crowes

Borne from the same blues-rock tree as Clapton and Aerosmith, Black Crowes guitarists Rich Robinson, Jeff Cease, and later Marc Ford, also found success mixing the major and minor pentatonic scales.

This first lick, over an A7 chord, is classic Crowes phrasing, with a nod to Joe Perry at the lick's close.

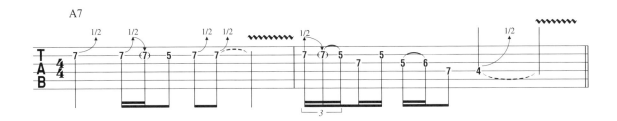

Here's another major-minor lick, similar to ones used by the Crowes' Jeff Cease as well as other blues-rockers such as Slash.

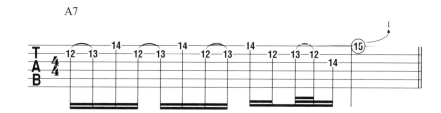

Here's an example of Jeff Cease in action as he mixes minor and major pentatonic scales in his solo to "Hard to Handle." Throughout this lick, Cease stands firmly planted in the mixed scale, as he highlights ♭7th and ♭3rd tones from the minor pentatonic scale while also managing to work 6th and major 3rd notes in from the major pentatonic scale.

"HARD TO HANDLE"
Black Crowes

Words and Music by Allen Jones,
Alvertis Bell and Otis Redding

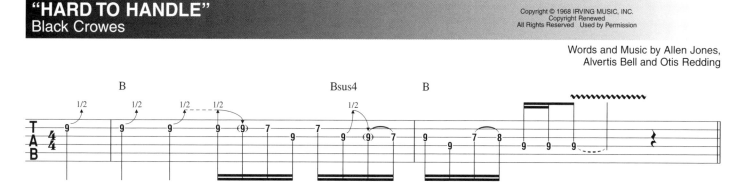

Robben Ford

Widely considered one of the top phraseologists in the game, Robben Ford often juxtaposes major and minor sounds in crafting his smooth, modern-blues lines.

Here's a Ford-style lick with plenty of major-minor rub, covering an A7–D7 progression.

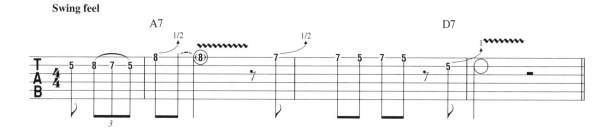

Ford is also quite capable of producing finger-twisting phrases with that major-minor juice. Here's one of those, this time over a G7 chord.

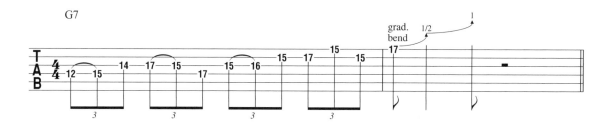

Here, Ford shows his stuff in a short interlude lick between verses of "Mama Talk to Your Daughter." Check out how Ford's first bend accesses major 3rd from a minor pentatonic shape; then, in the next measure, he bends up to a minor 3rd third from a major pentatonic shape. In both of these instances, he's accessed a scale tone from the other scale via his bend—slick!

"MAMA TALK TO YOUR DAUGHTER"
Robben Ford

Words and Music by J.B. Lenoir
and Alex Atkins

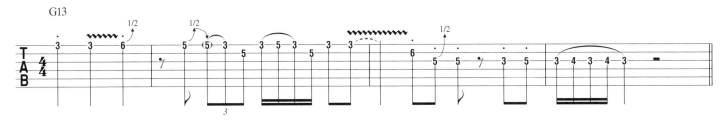

We've looked at a lot of major-minor pentatonic mixing in the blues-rock realm, but this technique stretched back to the blues masters of the previous era as well. Just to give you a taste, here's Freddie King mixing it up on a lick he plays in the solo to "Have You Ever Loved a Woman." We're in D♭ here, and over the V chord (A♭7), he darts up D♭ major pentatonic and climaxes with a high bend before toughening things up at the end of the measure by moving to the minor pentaonic. Though King recorded this back in 1960, his move from major to minor pentatonic at the end sounds just as fresh today.

"HAVE YOU EVER LOVED A WOMAN"
Freddie King

Words and Music by
Billy Myles

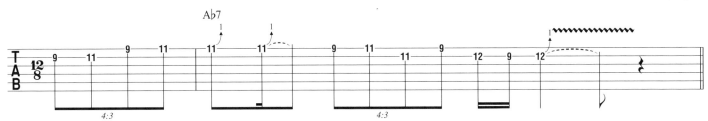

Next time you're jamming over a dominant chord, or especially when you come to that "Hendrix chord," remember some of the ideas you've leard in this lesson, and watch your phrases come to life.